Wedding Music
for
Classical Guitar

Arranged by
Christopher Boydston

1 2 3 4 5 6 7 8 9 0

Table of Contents

The Author—Christopher Boydston

"Bridal Chorus"

Arranged for the
Guitar by Christopher Boydston

Richard Wagner
(1813 - 1883)

3

(a.) After this chord, the less experienced Guitarist may skip to here ⊕

rit. _ _ _ _

4

"Wedding March"

(from a Midsummer Night's Dream)

Arranged for the Guitar
by Christopher Boydston

Felix Mendelssohn
(1809 - 1847)

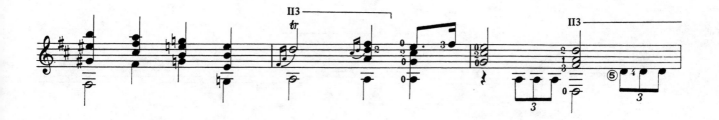

"Trumpet Tune"

Arranged for the
Guitar by Christopher Boydston

Henry Purcell
(1659 - 1695)

9

Gymnopédie #I

**Arranged for the Guitar
by Christopher Boydston**

Erik Satie
(1866 - 1925)

"Kemp's Jigge"

Arranged for the Guitar
by Christopher Boydston

An Anonymous Lute Piece
from the 17th Century

To Nanny

"Amazing Grace"

Arranged for the
Guitar by Christopher Boydston

To Ann

William Walker

"The Prince of Denmark's March"

("Trumpet Voluntary")

Arranged for the Guitar
by Christopher Boydston

Jeremiah Clarke
(1659 - 1707)

"The Prince of Denmark's March"
("Trumpet Voluntary")

Arranged for the Guitar
by Christopher Boydston

Jeremiah Clarke
(1659 - 1707)

* This version is intended for the more advanced player.

15

"From a Foreign Land," op. 15

**Arranged for the Guitar
by Christopher Boydston**

Robert Schumann
(1810 - 1856)

* These two measures are editorial.

"From a Foreign Land," Op. 15

Arranged for the Guitar
by Christopher Boydston

Robert Schumann
(1810 - 1856)

* This version is intended for the more advanced player.
** These two measures are editorial.

Prélude #1, op. 3

To My Parents

C. Boydston 1984

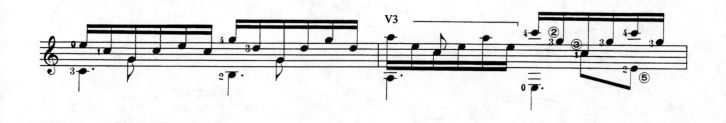

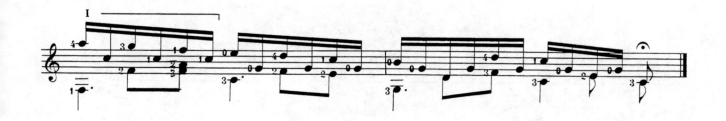

"Come Away"

Arranged for the
Guitar by Christopher Boydston

To Ann

John Dowland
(1563 - 1626)

"Jesu, Joy of Man's Desiring"

**Arranged for the Guitar
by Christopher Boydston**

J. S. Bach
(1685 - 1750)

Canon in D

Arranged for the Guitar
by Christopher Boydston

Johann Pachelbel
(1653 - 1706)